Alabama

BY MARI KESSELRING

The Child's World

Published by The Child's World®
1980 Lookout Drive • Mankato, MN 56003-1705
800-599-READ • www.childsworld.com

ACKNOWLEDGMENTS
The Child's World®: Mary Berendes, Publishing Director
The Design Lab: Design and production
Red Line Editorial: Editorial direction

PHOTO CREDITS: Juthathip Tybon/iStockphoto, cover, 1, 3; Matt Kania/Map
Hero, Inc., 4, 5; uniball/iStockphoto, 7; toddmedia/iStockphoto, 9; Andrew_
Howe/iStockphoto, 10; MIMOHE/iStockphoto, 11; dszc/iStockphoto, 13; AP
Images, 15; Rainier Ehrhardt/AP Images, 17; Library of Congress, 19; steve
estvanik/Shutterstock, 21; One Mile Up, 22; Quarter-dollar coin image from
the United States Mint, 22

LIBRARY OF CONGRESS CATALOGING-IN-PUBLICATION DATA
Kesselring, Mari.
  Alabama / by Mari Kesselring.
      p. cm.
Includes bibliographical references and index.
ISBN 978-1-60253-445-2 (library bound : alk. paper)
1. Alabama—Juvenile literature. I. Title.

F326.3.K47 2010
976.1—dc22

                              2010016160

Printed in the United States of America in Mankato, Minnesota.
July 2010
F11538

On the cover:
Alabama is
known as "the
Cotton State."

CONTENTS

Geography

Let's explore Alabama! Alabama is in the southern part of the United States. This area is called the South. Part of Alabama's southern border is the **Gulf** of Mexico.

TENNESSEE

MISSISSIPPI

GEORGIA

FLORIDA

Tuscumbia

Huntsville

Scottsboro

Fort Payne

ALABAMA

Birmingham

Moundville

Daviston

Alexander City

Selma

Tuskegee

Montgomery

Dothan

Mobile

Tombigbee River

Alabama River

Gulf of Mexico

NORTH
EAST
SOUTH
WEST

Cities

Montgomery is the capital of Alabama. Birmingham is the biggest city in the state. Another well-known city is Mobile. These cities have many old homes and **museums**.

Birmingham is home to about 230,000 people. ▶

Land

Alabama has mountains, forests, beaches, and **prairies**. The prairies are good for farming. Alabama has many rivers. Two are the Tombigbee River and the Alabama River. They both flow into the Gulf of Mexico.

Alabama forests turn colors in the fall. ▶

Plants and Animals

Alabama's many plants and animals enjoy the state's warm weather. The state bird is the yellowhammer. It is a type of **woodpecker**. The camellia is the state flower. It has many **petals**. They can be white, pink, or red.

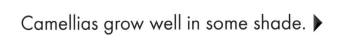

Camellias grow well in some shade. ▶

People and Work

More than 4 million people live in Alabama. Most people live and work in big cities. Some people also live in **rural** farm areas. Farmers here often raise chickens or grow cotton.

The rocket that took humans on their first trip to the moon was built in Alabama.

Cotton is an important crop for Alabama farmers. ▶

History

Native Americans have lived in the Alabama area for thousands of years. People from Europe settled in the area in the 1700s. Alabama became the twenty-second state in 1819. Some U.S. **Civil War** battles were fought here. Years later, the state was a main place for the **civil rights movement**. This helped black people gain equal rights.

Martin Luther King Jr. (front row, second from right) ▶
led a civil rights march to Montgomery in 1965.

Martin Luther King Jr. was a leader of the civil rights movement. He was a pastor in Montgomery.

Ways of Life

People in Alabama enjoy Mardi Gras early in the year. People enjoy colorful **parades** during the **festival**. Race car driving is a **popular** sport.

The Talladega Superspeedway is a famous racetrack in Alabama. ▶

Famous People

Rosa Parks was born in Alabama. She fought for equal rights. Jesse Owens was a fast runner who was born in this state. Singer Nat King Cole and author Helen Keller were born in Alabama, too.

When Rosa Parks refused to give up her bus seat to a white person in 1955, it drew attention to the civil rights movement.

Jesse Owens won four races at the 1936 Olympics. ▶

19

Famous Places

Visitors to Alabama can see battlefields from the Civil War. The Alabama War Memorial and Wall of Honor is here. It honors people from the state who have died in wars. The Azalea Trail in Mobile is another place to visit. People drive along the trail to see flower gardens and large houses.

Visitors to Alabama can see people act out Civil War battles. ▶

State Symbols

Seal

Alabama's rivers are shown on the state seal. Go to childsworld.com/links for a link to Alabama's state Web site, where you can get a firsthand look at the state seal.

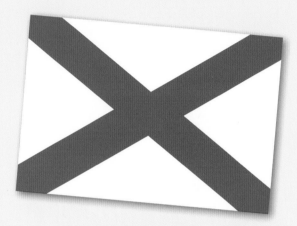

Flag

Alabama's state flag is similar to the flag used by the South during the Civil War.

Quarter

Helen Keller is on Alabama's state quarter. The quarter came out in 2003.

Glossary

civil rights movement (SIV-il RITES MOOV-munt): The civil rights movement is the name given to the struggle for equal rights for blacks in the United States during the 1950s and 1960s. Alabama was an important place in the civil rights movement.

Civil War (SIV-il WOR): In the United States, the Civil War was a war fought between the Northern and the Southern states from 1861 to 1865. Some Civil War battles were fought in Alabama.

festival (FESS-tih-vul): A festival is a celebration for an event or holiday. Mardi Gras is a festival.

gulf (GULF): A gulf is a large body of water with land around most of it. Part of Alabama borders the Gulf of Mexico.

museums (myoo-ZEE-umz): Museums are places where people go to see art, history, or science displays. Alabama has many museums to visit.

parades (puh-RAYDZ): Parades are when people march to honor holidays. Alabama has parades during Mardi Gras.

pastor (PASS-tur): A pastor is a leader of a church. Martin Luther King Jr. was a pastor in Alabama.

petals (PET-ulz): Petals are the colorful parts of flowers. The camellia, Alabama's state flower, has many petals.

popular (POP-yuh-lur): To be popular is to be enjoyed by many people. Race car driving is popular in Alabama.

prairies (PRAYR-eez): Prairies are flat or hilly grasslands. Alabama has prairies.

rural (ROOR-ul): Rural means having to do with the countryside. Many people live in rural areas of Alabama.

seal (SEEL): A seal is a symbol a state uses for government business. Alabama's state seal shows a map of the state.

symbols (SIM-bulz): Symbols are pictures or things that stand for something else. The seal and flag are Alabama's symbols.

woodpecker (WOOD-pek-er): A woodpecker is a bird that finds food by making holes in tree bark with its beak. The yellowhammer, Alabama's state bird, is a type of woodpecker.

Further Information

Books

Crane, Carol. *Y is for Yellowhammer: An Alabama Alphabet*. Chelsea, MI: Sleeping Bear Press, 2003.

Feeney, Kathy. *Alabama*. New York: Children's Press, 2008.

Martin, Michael A. *Alabama: The Heart of Dixie*. Milwaukee, WI: World Almanac Library, 2002.

Web Sites

Visit our Web site for links about Alabama: *childsworld.com/links*

Note to Parents, Teachers, and Librarians: We routinely verify our Web links to make sure they are safe and active sites. So encourage your readers to check them out!

Index